WHAT IF YOU

Animal Home!?

by **Sandra Markle**

Illustrated by
Howard McWilliam

Scholastic Inc.

For Rachel Bragg and the children of Ranch Heights Elementary in Bartlesville, Oklahoma

A special thank-you to Skip Jeffery for his loving support during the creative process.

The author would like to thank the following people for sharing their enthusiasm and expertise: Richard A. Beausoleil, Washington Department of Fish & Wildlife, Wenatchee, Washington (Black Bear); Dr. Winifred Frick, Bat Conservation International, Austin, Texas (Mexican Free-tailed Bat); Dr. Glynnis A. Hood, University of Alberta, Augustana Campus, Camrose, Alberta, Canada (Beaver); Dr. Laura A. Kelley, University of Exeter, Cornwall, United Kingdom (Great Bowerbird); Dr. Samuel Ocko, Stanford University, Stanford, California (Mound-building Termites); Dr. Simon Pollard, University of Canterbury, Christchurch, New Zealand (Honeybee, Orb Weaver Spider); Dr. James Rimmer, University of St. Andrews, St. Andrews, Fife, Scotland, United Kingdom (Hermit Crab); Dr. Craig M. Shuttleworth, Bangor University, Bangor, Wales, United Kingdom (Gray Squirrel); Dr. Ariana Strandburg-Peshkin, University of Konstanz and Max Planck Institute of Animal Behavior, Konstanz, Germany (Meerkat); Dr. René E. van Dijk, Sweco, Netherlands B.V., the Netherlands (Sociable Weaver Bird); Dr. Lindsay Welfelt, Washington Department of Fish & Wildlife, Wenatchee, Washington (Black Bear)

Photos ©: cover top and throughout: Dim Dimich/Shutterstock; cover center: MagicBloods/Shutterstock; back cover: Angela Waye/Shutterstock; 4: Bob Hilscher/Shutterstock; 4 inset: Erlend Haarberg/NPL/Minden Pictures; 6: David Hosking/Alamy Stock Photo; 6 inset: Jason Edwards/Getty Images; 8: Gerard Lacz/VWPics/Alamy Stock Photo; 8 inset: Ingo Arndt/Minden Pictures; 10: Karine Aigner/NPL/Minden Pictures; 10 inset: Karine Aigner/NPL/Minden Pictures; 12: De Klerk/Alamy Stock Photo; 12 inset: Ann and Steve Toon/Alamy Stock Photo; 14: David Juan/Getty Images; 14 inset: WorldFoto/Alamy Stock Photo; 16: Ingo Arndt/Minden Pictures; 16 inset: Andrew Watson/Alamy Stock Photo; 18: Sunshower Shots/Getty Images; 18 inset: Nature Picture Library/Alamy Stock Photo; 20: Itsik Marom/Alamy Stock Photo; 20 inset: SeaTops/Alamy Stock Photo; 22: Gina Dittmer/Alamy Stock Photo; 22 inset: David Mabe/Alamy Stock Photo; 24: Nature Picture Library/Alamy Stock Photo; 24 inset: critterbiz/Shutterstock; 30 top: vovashevchuk/Getty Images; 30 center: Tuul & Bruno Morandi/Getty Images; 30 bottom: David Wall/Alamy Stock Photo; 31 top: Apurva Madia/Alamy Stock Photo; 31 center: Stephen Foote/Alamy Stock Photo; 31 bottom: imageBROKER/Alamy Stock Photo.

Text copyright © 2024 by Sandra Markle
Illustrations copyright © 2024 by Howard McWilliam

Library of Congress Cataloging-in-Publication Data available

ISBN 978-1-339-01485-2 (paperback)
ISBN 978-1-339-04905-2 (library binding)

10 9 8 7 6 5 4 3 2 1   24 25 26 27 28

Printed in China 38
First edition, May 2024

Book design by Kay Petronio

What if one day when you woke up, your room looked a little bit strange? And you discovered that the home you live in was now VERY different? What if an animal's home had taken its place?

BEAVER

A beaver's lodge is its home. First, it piles up mud and rocks. Next, it gnaws branches off trees and heaps a BIG mound atop this base. The beaver chews several underwater entrances into this mound. Inside, it hollows out a living space. Leafy bedding makes it a cozy home for raising kits (baby beavers).

FACT

A beaver's building tools are its big, sharp incisors (front teeth). These have a superhard coating and never stop growing so a beaver can keep gnawing.

If you had a
beaver's home,
doing homework would
be muddy fun!

5

GREAT BOWERBIRD

A male great bowerbird's bower is his home. But it's only while he is competing in the annual BEST BOWER contest. First, he creates a twig mat. Into this, he pokes tall sticks to form a walkway for displaying pebbles and colorful objects. Each female chooses and mates with her BEST BOWER winner. Then she builds a tree-nest home and raises the pair's chicks (baby birds) .

FACT

A male great bowerbird steals from other males to make sure his bower is the GREATEST.

If you had a male great bowerbird's home, you'd be the neighborhood decorating contest's BIGGEST winner ever.

HONEYBEE

A honeybee's hive is its home. A hive has lots of six-sided rooms called cells. Honeybees need a big home to store enough honey and pollen to feed everyone. The queen bee produces as many as 2,000 eggs a day to keep the family growing. And every larva (baby bee) gets its own cell with nurse bees on duty for care and feeding.

FACT

Young worker bees produce tiny slivers of wax. Older worker bees collect these to build and repair the hive's cells.

If you had a honeybee's home, you'd have your own room—plus room service.

MEXICAN FREE-TAILED BAT

A Mexican free-tailed bat's cave is its home. It shares this space with lots of other bats—sometimes millions! All day, it stays home and rests. At night, it exits the cave and swoops through the air, eating all the flying insects it catches. When females have *pups* (baby bats), they leave them home while they go out to eat. Upon returning, each female follows its own pup's calls to find it again.

FACT

A Mexican free-tailed bat sleeps hanging upside down, using its toe claws to grip and hold on tight.

If you had a Mexican free-tailed bat's home, it would be a great place to hang out with friends.

SOCIABLE WEAVER BIRD

A sociable weaver bird's nest is its home. They live there year-round. More than 100 birds may live together and share in building the nest. First, they make a roof of large twigs and dry grasses. Underneath, in what looks like a haystack, the birds make their own homes. Like an apartment building, each home has a short tunnel leading into a cozy 6-inch-wide chamber. Every year, sociable weaver birds repair and expand their shared home.

FACT

Sociable weaver birds build the world's BIGGEST tree nests. They can be 20 feet wide and 10 feet tall.

If you had a sociable weaver bird's home, you'd always have friends next door!

13

MEERKAT

A meerkat's underground burrow is its home. This network of tunnels and chambers may spread out 200 feet and have 100 entrances. Meerkats usually live in groups and share the burrow-digging work. They may also have 20 or more burrows. So, home is always nearby. And if a jackal or other predator comes close, a meerkat easily pops home and stays safe.

FACT

When meerkat pups are born, the group sticks to one burrow for about three weeks. Adults take turns skipping daytime feeding to babysit.

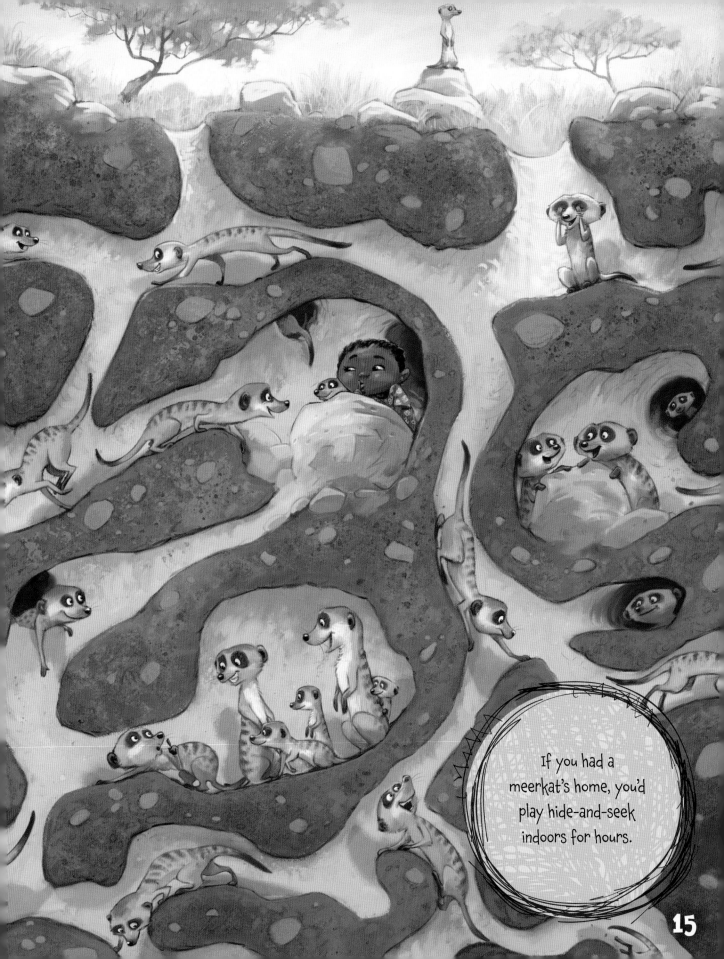

If you had a meerkat's home, you'd play hide-and-seek indoors for hours.

15

MOUND-BUILDING TERMITE

A mound-building termite's underground nest is its home. It lives there with its family. There is an egg-laying queen, larvae (baby termites), males, soldiers, and millions of workers. The workers build the nest. As they make the nest's underground chambers and passageways, they carry the waste dirt up and out. Their dump becomes the mound.

FACT

The average mound-building termite mound is 9 feet tall. But some in Australia are 26 feet tall!

If you had a mound-building termite's home, you'd easily shape your bedroom into the room of your dreams.

GRAY SQUIRREL

A gray squirrel's drey is its home. It builds high up on a strong tree branch. Snipping off twigs with its sharp front teeth, it makes a platform. Using more twigs, it weaves the sides and roof. When finished, the drey is basketball-sized with a flap-like door. But one drey is not enough. It builds four or five so good food sources are always close to home.

FACT

A gray squirrel keeps rain and wind out by coating its drey with moss and leaves.

If you had a gray squirrel's home, you'd build an amazing treehouse fort.

HERMIT CRAB

A hermit crab's shell is its home. It needs it to cover its rear end—the only part of its body lacking a shell-like coat. Though a shell it finds may be a great fit, it's never the perfect home. So, a hermit crab checks out every empty shell it comes across. It may switch shells or keep its old home until it grows and needs one that's bigger. Or until it spots another shell.

FACT

Some hermit crabs stick sea anemones on their shell. Their stinging tentacles help keep hermit crabs from being fish food.

If you had a hermit crab's home, you'd have shelter wherever you go.

ORB WEAVER SPIDER

An orb weaver spider's web is its home. It's also a midair trap. To create it, the spider produces different kinds of silk—some dry, some sticky. First, the orb weaver spins its web's frame with dry silk. Next, it builds a spiral of sticky silk, creating the web's net. Now the spider can be sure any insect that visits its home stays for dinner. YUMMY!

FACT

An orb weaver spider shoots bands of silk over prey that lands in its web. Then it wraps this up to dine on later.

If you had
an orb weaver
spider's home, you'd
never have a
surprise visitor.

BLACK BEAR

A black bear's den is its home. But it only spends winters there. It may be a home it has used before or a new home it finds or digs. Before settling, a black bear carries in leaves and grasses to make a bed. Males den alone but females share with cubs. A black bear will quickly wake to face danger. But left alone, it snoozes till spring.

FACT

Black bear cubs are born in January. They will be big enough to go into the world come spring.

If you had
a black bear's home,
you'd only spend the winter
there. But you'd be so comfy
you'd stay for months . . .
and months . . .
and months.

Having an animal's home could be cool for a while.

So, if you could stay for more than a day, which home would be right for you?

Luckily, you don't have to choose. You will always live where people live.

People who live in some of Earth's most challenging places have very special homes. They are built to keep people who live there safely sheltered.

AN IGLOO is a home for cold, frozen parts of Alaska, Canada, and the Arctic. Building materials are available after each snowfall. And it makes a good temporary shelter from blizzards.

A YURT is a sturdy home just right for very windy parts of Central Asia, such as Mongolia. It has an easy-to-take-apart wood frame. And it is covered with layers of wool, felt, or other fabric. For families tending grazing animals, it lets them take their home along wherever they travel.

A DUGOUT is a home built by digging into hillsides by people living in Coober Pedy, Australia. The soil there is stable enough to make large rooms. And by being underground, the residents escape hot summer days and cold winter nights.

A ROCK-CUT HOME is a natural for people living with easy-to-carve rock formations like those in Cappadocia, Turkey. Building and living in these homes is believed to date back to ancient times. Sometimes, even the tables and beds are carved out of the rock.

A MUDHIF is a house built of dried reeds on top of a floating reed island. It's the perfect home for the marshes of southern Iraq. Construction starts by cutting reeds and making long bundles. These are bent and tied together, forming arches. Woven mats laid over the reed beams form the roof and walls.

A TURF HOUSE is a kind of home built in Iceland since ancient times. Turf is grass plus a layer of dirt. A turf house is built with turf blocks set on a supporting wood frame. Turf is such good insulation that the house stays cool in summer and warm in winter.

OTHER BOOKS IN THE SERIES

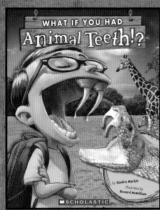

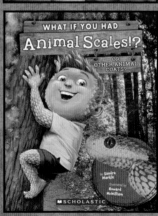

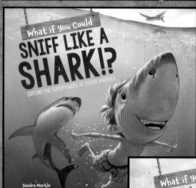

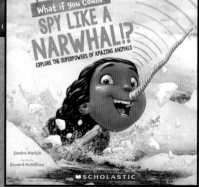